HOW TO SPEAK FOOTBALL

Also by Sally Cook, with illustrations by Ross MacDonald

How to Speak Baseball:
An Illustrated Guide to Ballpark Banter

How to Speak Golf:
An Illustrated Guide to Links Lingo

In memory of Dr. Daniel Williams

Special thanks to:
Michael Globetti,
Diane McWhorter, and Daniel Williams

HOW to SPEAK

FOOTBALL

SALLY COOK and **ROSS MACDONALD**

From Ankle Breaker to Zebra:
An Illustrated Guide to
Gridiron Gab

FLATIRON
BOOKS

www.flatironbooks.com

The Library of Congress Cataloging-in-Publication Data is
available upon request.

ISBN 978-1-250-07199-6 (paper over board)
ISBN 978-1-250-07200-9 (e-book)

Designed by Mike Gmitter

Our books may be purchased in bulk for promotional,
educational, or business use. Please contact your local
bookseller or the Macmillan Corporate and Premium Sales
Department at (800) 221-7945, extension 5442, or by e-mail
at MacmillanSpecialMarkets@macmillan.com.

First Edition: September 2016

10 9 8 7 6 5 4 3 2 1

INTRODUCTION

Over the years professional football has consistently been ranked in the polls as the most popular spectator sport in the United States. In fact, the Super Bowl, which is the championship of American football, is practically considered a national holiday. And college football is ranked third in the polls behind only professional football and baseball.

Listening to an announcer call a game without an understanding of the lexicon can be frustrating and bewildering, to say the least. Appreciating and enjoying the game means being conversant with the lingo.

When the announcer says something about a "Hail Mary," is he talking about a church event or a play out on the field? When mentioning a "zebra" or a "wildcat formation," is the commentator referring to a zoo or perhaps a safari or is he simply observing something on the gridiron? When he says, "blitz," "formation," or "bomb," does he mean a far-off war zone or is he still speaking football?

Here we've answered those questions and many more, while providing you with some basics. By collecting our favorite terms, team names, players' nicknames, and entertaining historical facts and events and pairing them with amusing illustrations we hope to have you speaking football like a pro in no time.

ALLIGATOR ARMS

Coaches, players, and television commentators frequently use this term to describe—and disparage—a would-be receiver who keeps his arms protectively tucked in close to his ribs instead of stretched out to catch the ball. The would-be receiver senses a tackler bearing down on him and is more focused on protecting himself from the hard hit than catching the ball.

ANKLE BREAKER

When a player speedily changes directions, causing another player to become so off balance that he falls.

AUDIBLE

A play called by the quarterback at the line of scrimmage to make a change from the play that was originally called in the huddle. Also known as check off.

BACKFIELD

The area behind the line of scrimmage, where the fullbacks and halfbacks line up and the quarterback passes from. Also the collective expression for running backs and fullbacks.

ANKLE BREAKER

BITE

BELLY

When a running back runs the ball up the middle of the field after taking a simple handoff from the quarterback.

BIG UGLIES

Offensive linemen. No pun intended.

BITE

When a defender falls for a fake or false pass.

BLACK MONDAY

The day after the final Sunday of the National Football League season (Week 17) when many coaches and general managers of floundering teams are fired or resign their positions.

BLIND SIDE

The side of the offensive line that the quarterback is facing away from when he drops back to pass or stands in the backfield looking for a receiver. For right-handed quarterbacks (as 95 percent of all quarterbacks happen to be), the left tackle protects the blind side. Extra emphasis is placed on keeping the quarterback's blind side safe.

Continued on page 16

SIDELINES: 1ST AND 10 — DO IT AGAIN

Totally new to football? If so, understanding the distinguishing characteristic of a "down"—a period in which a play occurs—is mandatory. Here's how it works: The team in possession of the football has a total of four downs to progress ten yards or more toward their opponent's goal line. If they fail to advance that far, control of the ball is turned over to the other team. In most circumstances, if a team gets to their final down, they will punt to their opponent, which forces them to begin their drive from farther down the field. If they are close enough, they might also try to score a field goal.

A down starts with a snap or free kick and ends when the ball or the player in possession of it is declared down by an official, a team scores, or the ball or player in possession of it leaves the field of play. The player with possession of the ball after he has been tackled or is otherwise unable to advance the ball farther on account of the play having ended is down. Also "down" may refer to the ball after it is made dead in one way or another. The line of scrimmage for the next play will be determined by the position of the ball when it is down.

Each possession begins with a first down. The line to gain is marked 10 yards downfield from the start of this possession, and the position is described as "1st and 10." If the goal line is less than 10 yards downfield, then the goal line is the line to gain and the situation is "1st and goal." If the offensive team moves the ball past the line to gain, they make a new first down. If they fail to do this after four downs possession of the ball returns to the opposing team at the place where the ball was downed at the end of the last down.

If a penalty against the defensive team moves the ball past the line to gain, the offensive team gets a new first down. Some defensive penalties give the offense an automatic first down regardless of the distance.

What if the offensive team has not yet made a first down before reaching the final down? The team then faces a last down situation or fourth down situation where the team is forced to decide whether to scrimmage the ball in an attempt to pick up the first down or alternatively to kick the ball, either by punting or making a field goal attempt. Playing more aggressively is usually seen as the better option, but kicking the ball is normally viewed as the safer solution.

Downing the player with possession of the ball is one way to end a play. Other methods include the player with the ball going out of bounds, an incomplete pass, or a score. Usually a player is made down when he is tackled by the defense. In the NFL, if the offensive player touches the ground with a part of his body other than his hands or feet, then he is down if any defensive player touches him. In college football, an offensive player touching the ground in the same way is down, regardless of whether a defensive player touches him.

A player may down the ball by dropping to one knee if he is recovering the ball in the opponent's end zone following a kickoff. A player in possession of the ball will down the ball if he fumbles it out of bounds. If a QB or any ball carrier is running with the ball during his initial possession of the same play following the snap, he may down the ball by voluntarily sliding from his feet to a sitting or reclining position. This is done to protect the player from injury.

SIDELINES: PLAYERS' NICKNAMES

WILLIAM PERRY played college football for Clemson University and was recognized as an All-American. In 1985, he was selected in the first round of the draft and played professionally for the Chicago Bears and the Philadelphia Eagles. Perry weighed in at 200 pounds by the time he was eleven years old. As a freshman at Clemson in 1981, he earned his nickname "The Refrigerator" or "The Fridge" when fellow player Ray Brown could barely squeeze into an elevator with Perry and their laundry. Brown said, "Man, you're about as big as a refrigerator." Perry's Super Bowl ring size—25—is the largest of any professional football player. For comparison: The average adult male wears a ring size between 10 and 12.

Continued from page 9

because he can't see the coming impact. Teams will often put their best offensive lineman on the blind side.

BLITZ

A defensive ploy where additional players are sent into the opponent's backfield to try to tackle the quarterback or upset his pass attempt, or to disrupt a running play by making the play unfold prematurely. Derived from the word *blitzkrieg*, the German strategy of "lightning war" employed during World War II.

BOMB

Long pass completion. A play often used at the start of a game or when the team is behind at the very end of a game. It does not necessarily result in a touchdown. Also called deep post, fly pattern, skinny post.

BOOTLEG

A trick play where the quarterback runs with the ball in the direction of either sideline behind the line of scrimmage. The quarterback may then fake a handoff (to a running back) and

BOMB

continue running toward the end zone, and may be accompanied by an offensive lineman blocking for him. The bootleg is called to confuse the opposing team's defense by moving the quarterback away from where he is expected to be, directly behind center. The bootleg and variations on this play (including the naked bootleg, where the QB is alone on his run, thus "naked" without supporting offensive linemen) have been more frequently used in recent years. This is because the rules have changed allowing a quarterback to avoid a sack by throwing the ball away once he is outside the area between where the two offensive tackles line up prior to the snap. Since in a bootleg the quarterback normally sets up to throw well outside the tackles, if he is in danger of getting sacked he can throw the ball out of bounds without risking an intentional grounding penalty.

The name "bootleg" derives from the fact that on a play action the quarterback often holds the football by his thigh to hide it from the defense and make the run look credible, resembling what bootleggers looked like when they hid whiskey in their pants during Prohibition.

BUMP AND RUN

A pass defense tactic. The defender bumps the receiver coming off the line of scrimmage, then covers him in stride downfield. Defenders may only bump the receiver in the first 5 yards forward from the line of scrimmage.

CADENCE

The quarterback's rhythm or tempo when calling out signals.

CENTER

The player who snaps the ball to the quarterback. He handles the ball on every play.

CHAIN GANG

The officials on the sideline who hold the yardage and down markers. Also called a chain crew.

CHEAT SHEET

A plastic-encased play card that the quarterback wears on his wrist to crib plays from.

SIDELINES: PLAYERS' NICKNAMES

JOE NAMATH, an American Football League icon and former quarterback, played college football for the University of Alabama under coach Paul "Bear" Bryant from 1962 to 1964. During the mid-'60s and '70s he played for the New York Jets and in 1967 became the first quarterback to pass for more than 4,000 yards on one season. He finished his career with the Los Angeles Rams in 1977 and was elected to the Hall of Fame in 1985. Sherman Plunkett, a Jets teammate, gave Namath the nickname "Broadway Joe" because of his love of New York nightlife and because he dabbled in acting on television and in the movies. The nickname "Joe Willie Namath," his full given name, was popularized by sportscaster Howard Cosell. Namath began the fad of wearing a full-length fur coat on the sidelines, which was embraced by many players after him. The NFL has since banned this, requiring all team personnel (players, coaches, athletic trainers, etc.) to wear league-approved team apparel. Namath also stood out from other AFL and NFL players by wearing low-cut white football shoes instead of the traditional black high-tops, earning him the nickname "Joe Willie Whiteshoes." Today the NFL often fines players for not wearing shoes that match those of their teammates.

CHEESEHEADS

The nickname for the legions of Green Bay Packers fans worldwide, acknowledging Wisconsin's abundant cheese production. First heard as an insult at a 1987 baseball game between the Chicago White Sox and Milwaukee Brewers, it soon became a source of pride. Since 1994 the nickname has been embraced by Packers fans and team owners (and even their pets) who wear bright yellow foam cheese-wedge hats wherever the team plays or in the comfort of their own living rooms across the country when Green Bay is making its weekly televised appearance.

CHOP BLOCK

An attempt by an offensive player to block at the thigh level or lower.

CLIP/CLIPPING

When a player throws his body across the leg of an eligible receiver; or when a player charges or falls into the back of an opponent below his waist after approaching him from behind, specifically if the opponent is not a runner; or after a block, a player rolls up on the legs of an opponent.

CHEESEHEADS

This is a penalty that can cost a team 15 yards. If committed by the defense, it is an automatic first down as well.

COFFIN CORNER

The strategic starting field position spot for the defense directly in front of the end zone, inside the 5-yard line. Originates from the "coffin corner" found in many Victorian houses describing a decorative niche, or very small "corner," cut into the wall of a staircase landing. A successful coffin corner kick goes out of bounds just before the orange pylon denoting the end zone. The punter, who needs to have a high level of skill for this kick, tries to place the ball so that it lands out of bounds or is downed on the field by another member of the kicking team anywhere inside the 5-yard line without touching the goal line. This forces a difficult field position for the receiving team on their ensuing possession.

CORNERBACK

A defensive player (who must be quick and agile) aligned at the corner of the field. Assigned to cover the wide receiver of the offensive team.

COUNTER

A play where the offense runs the ball in the opposite direction, which is contrary to what the defense expects.

CRACKBACK BLOCK

When a wide receiver comes from the outside and blocks to the inside on a running play. Considered dangerous because the blocker is blocking down in the opposite direction of the flow of play, thus often catching a defender by surprise. Blocking below the waist on a crackback is illegal and regularly elicits a penalty.

CRACKBACK BLOCK

DEFENSIVE END

DEFENSIVE END

Usually the outermost players on either end of the defensive line. Their jobs are twofold: Ordinarily they are tasked with overcoming offensive blocking to meet in the backfield where they combine to tackle the quarterback or ball carrier. On running plays to the outside, they are responsible for forcing the ball carrier either out of bounds or toward (into) the pursuit of their defensive teammates.

DEFENSIVE TACKLE

The inner two members of the defensive line. They are supposed to maintain their positions in order to stop a running play or run through a gap in the offensive line to pressure the quarterback or upset the backfield formation.

DIME

When the defense removes a linebacker or defensive lineman and replaces him with a sixth defensive back. Only used in obvious passing situations. Similar to a prevent defense and nickel defense.

DINK AND DUNK
A short passing game. A series of short passes (usually less than 5 yards) that lead to first downs and use up the clock. Frustrates a defense.

DIVE PLAY
A quick handoff run up the middle where the offense needs only a short distance to gain a first down or touchdown.

DOUBLING UP/DOUBLE-TEAMING
Two defenders covering one receiver.

DOWN BY CONTACT
In college football, a ball carrier is considered down by contact when his knee touches the ground, whether he was tackled or went down without being touched by an opposing player, ending the play in either case. However, in the NFL, a ball carrier needs to be touched by an opposing player to be considered down by contact. The one exception: If an NFL quarterback runs then slides to the turf feet first, "surrendering his body" before contact occurs, he is considered down where the slide began.

DRAG ROUTE

The path taken by a receiver where he runs a few yards downfield, then turns 90 degrees toward the center of the field and runs parallel to the line of scrimmage and "underneath" typical secondary coverage. Also called in route.

DRAW

When the quarterback drops back in the pocket pretending to pass only to hand the ball off to a running back or run the ball himself on a designed play.

DRAW

SIDELINES: COLDEST GAME IN NFL HISTORY

THE ICE BOWL

With temperatures plunging to -13°F (-25°C), the coldest game in NFL history was played on December 31, 1967, between the Green Bay Packers and Dallas Cowboys at Lambeau Field in Green Bay, Wisconsin. It was so frigid that when the referee blew the whistle at kickoff it froze to his lips. Players grumbled that the field was like a sheet of ice and that the football felt like a hard rock. The Packers won 21–17, eventually going on to win Super Bowl II against the Oakland Raiders.

THE FREEZER BOWL

A little more than thirteen years later, on January 10, 1982, a game was played in what was the coldest temperature in NFL history in terms of wind chill. Dubbed the Freezer Bowl, the game took place at Cincinnati's Riverfront Stadium between the San Diego Chargers and the Cincinnati Bengals in front of 46,300 frozen fans. While the air temperature was a mere -9°F (-23°C), it felt more like -59°F (-50°C) when you factored in the 35 mile per hour winds.

The Bengals' offensive line played the entire game with bare arms. Several of them, including the quarterbacks for both teams, played with bare hands as well. Some of the players placed hot water bottles inside their cups (athletic supporters) and between plays they walked around with their hands in their pants! Less than one week later the Chargers thawed out—playing in an overtime game in Miami in 88°F (31°C) high-humidity weather.

END ZONE

The scoring area on the field, between the end line and goal line bordered by the sidelines. There are two end zones, each being on an opposite end of the field, bordered on all sides by a white line indicating its beginning and end points, with orange, square pylons.

FAIR CATCH

A signal the kick returner gives by waving his extended arm, side to side. The opposition must give him an uninterrupted opportunity to field the football when he does this. This rule protects receivers because their attention is on fielding the ball, making them vulnerable to injurious hits. Once the player fields the ball, the play is blown dead and the spot on the field where he caught it becomes the starting point for the offensive drive.

FG

Abbreviation for field goal. A play where the ball is placekicked through the goalposts. Scores three points for the kicking team.

FIELD POSITION

Where the football is located on the 100 yards of

the field when the play starts. It is important for teams to be attentive to this because they play differently based on what yard line they start a play on.

FIRST DOWN
Making the 10 yards a team needs to get a new set of 4 downs.

FLAG PATTERN
The course that a wide receiver runs where he starts running straight downfield, then turns and runs diagonally toward the back corner of the end zone.

FLAG PATTERN

FLANKER

A receiver on the offensive team whose position is toward the side and behind the line of scrimmage. A little-used position that has now been superseded by slot receiver.

FLEA-FLICKER

A trick play where the quarterback hands the ball off to the running back straight up the middle. The running back then stops in his tracks and tosses the ball back to the quarterback behind him who then throws the ball deep downfield to a receiver. The play is intended to fool the defensive team into thinking that a play is a run instead of a pass. This is an extreme alternative of the play action pass and an extension of the halfback option play.

FLOOD

Many receivers in the same area of the field.

FLEA-FLICKER

FUMBLE

FRONT FOUR

The four defensive players positioned on the line of scrimmage in a common defensive alignment to guard against the run and to rush the passer. The primary run stoppers.

FRONT SEVEN

A defensive alignment that might include three linemen and four linebackers, or the now standard 4-3 arrangement: four linemen and three linebackers.

FULLBACK

The offensive back closer to the scrimmage line when there are several backs in a formation. Generally used as a blocker for the running back or quarterback but can also carry the ball and catch passes. Fullbacks, who are generally bigger than running backs, are short-yardage runners.

FUMBLE

When a ball carrier loses the football that had been under his control during a play.

SIDELINES: HOTTEST GAME IN NFL HISTORY

The hottest temperature ever recorded in an NFL game was 130°F (54°C) on September 19, 1971. The game was played at Tulane Stadium in New Orleans between the New Orleans Saints and Los Angeles Rams. It was the fifty-second NFL season opener and Archie Manning's NFL debut. The heat-absorbing AstroTurf had just been installed at the stadium, raising the temperature even higher. The Saints won the game against the heavily favored Rams, 24–20, thanks to the 1-yard touchdown run by the hot new star Archie Manning.

FUMBLEROOSKI

A trick play where the quarterback deliberately places or leaves the ball on the ground upon receiving it from the center, technically fumbling it. The backs run to the right, and the right guard picks up the ball and runs inside defensive pursuit to the left, with this deceit often convincing enough to produce a touchdown. Although the NCAA banned the play following the 1992 season and the NFL considers it a "forward fumble," making it illegal, variations of the play's general strategy are still sometimes used.

GADGET PLAY

A play designed to trick the defense. Often risky, it offers the potential for a large gain or a touchdown if it is successful, but with the chance of a significant loss of yards or turnover if it isn't. Also called flea-flicker, gimmick play, trick play.

GRIDIRON

Refers to either the field or the game of football. In North America, however, it is mostly used to indicate the field, usually in a somewhat symbolic or lyrical sense. Originated as a description of the playing field, which was marked with a series of parallel lines resembling a gridiron. That system was discarded in the 1930s in favor of a system of yard lines and hash marks used today.

GUNNER

Typically the fastest player on the team who can be used for his speed on the outside of the line of scrimmage when a team drops into punt formation, and subsequently covers the punt downfield.

GUNNER

HAIL MARY

A long forward pass that's a last-ditch attempt to complete a touchdown, with only a small chance of success, especially at or near the end of a half or the end of the game.

HANDS TO THE FACE

A penalty when a defender illegally uses his hands to gain leverage and strikes an offensive player's face mask or gets his hands beneath the face mask and in contact with an opponent's head or face. Didn't Mother always say, "Keep your hands to yourself!"?

HANG TIME

The length of time that a punt stays in the air. For the punting team, longer is better because the tacklers have more time to get downfield and cover the punt either by tackling an opposing returner or downing the football if it is not fielded or fair-caught. The combination of a long punt with a long hang time is usually the ideal change of possession for the punting team.

HANDS TO THE FACE

SIDELINES: TEAM NAMES

JACKSONVILLE JAGUARS

Black panthers are native to Florida, but jaguars aren't. Nevertheless, North America's oldest living jaguar resided in the Jacksonville Zoo in December 1991 when fans voted for the football team to be named after the zoo's cool cat. The other choices—Sharks and Stingrays—were doused.

MINNESOTA VIKINGS

Naming a team for not one, but two cities presents a challenge. Fortunately, Minnesota has only one NFL team, so it was possible to name the team for the entire state. Given the Scandinavian origins of many Minnesotans, Vikings, albeit with different-style helmets, were a natural, don't cha know.

NEW ORLEANS SAINTS

On the field, football players are no saints, but in jazz-crazed New Orleans, where the unofficial anthem is "When the Saints Go Marching In," the team name—derived from the song—is appropriate. Despite the name, the players wear helmets, not halos.

NEW YORK JETS

Originally called the Titans, the team went bankrupt in 1962 and the new owners needed a new name, one that was not associated with the un-Titan-like collapse. Some other names that were considered were: Dodgers, which was nixed by the baseball team; Gothams, which they worried would likely morph into Goths (the ill-behaving European raiders); and Boros, after the city's boroughs, but could also likely morph into Burro and then Jackass. The Jets were chosen in recognition of their stadium's proximity to LaGuardia Airport, as fans are regularly reminded since the takeoff path is almost directly over the stadium.

PHILADELPHIA EAGLES

Originally the Frankford Yellowjackets, the new owners, who purchased the team in 1933, decided to take the sting out of the old name. Drawing inspiration from the insignia of the centerpiece of President Franklin D. Roosevelt's New Deal, specifically the National Recovery Act's "blue eagle," they named the new franchise the Philadelphia Eagles.

THE BALTIMORE RAVENS

Named after Edgar Allen Poe's "The Raven," the new name was chosen in 1996 from the results of a poll conducted by *The Baltimore Sun*. Poe wrote this poem, one of his most famous, while living in Baltimore in the 1830s. The team's mascots are aptly named Edgar, Allan, and Poe!

SIDELINES: PLAYERS' NICKNAMES

MIKE DITKA, a former player, coach, and television commentator, earned a variety of nicknames throughout his career, such as "Iron Mike" because of his gritty personality and the fact that he grew up in a Pennsylvania steel town. As a tight end for the Bears in the 1960s, he was called "The Hammer" because he didn't just stiff-arm would-be tacklers, he clubbed them. Ditka coached the Chicago Bears for eleven years and the New Orleans Saints for three and became known as "Da Coach," as a nod to his midwestern accent. One of only two people to win a Super Bowl as a player, an assistant coach, and a coach—Ditka is the only person in modern history to win the championship as both a player and coach with the same team.

HARD COUNT

A quarterback's ploy to get the defense to jump offside by calling out one sound or word more forcefully than the others during his cadence. The best QBs who rely on this are almost Shakespearean in carrying out the ploy. Hard counts are not used often because they can also make the quarterback's own linemen jump early and draw a false-start penalty.

HASHMARKS

Two rows of lines near the middle of the field parallel to the sidelines. These approximately 1-yard-long lines are used to mark each of the 5-yard lines, which go from sideline to sideline. All plays start with the ball on or between the hash marks. If the ball is downed in between a hash mark and the nearest sideline, it must be reset on the hash mark for the next play.

HIKE

A snap from the center to the quarterback.

HITCH

A portion of a pass route that causes a defender

to stumble. Often it will be caused by a faked stop by the receiver, who then continues on to another part of the field.

HITTING THE HOLE
When a ball carrier quickly finds an opening to run through at the line of scrimmage.

HOLDING
One of the most common penalties in football, this is when a player grabs another player to gain an advantage. The penalty can be called on the offense or defense. Offensive holding is assessed 10 yards from the previous line of scrimmage. Defensive holding is assessed 5 yards from the previous line of scrimmage, and the offense is given a first down.

HOOK AND LATERAL
When a receiver runs a pass route where he "buttonhooks" at the end of the route, catches a short pass from the quarterback, then before the defense can tackle him, almost instantly flips or laterals the ball back to a teammate who is trailing him. Once he has possession of the football, he has a better chance of eluding tacklers than the

HOT READ

original receiver. A trick play also known as the hook-and-ladder play.

HOT READ

When a quarterback sees a blitz coming and hastily passes to a receiver running a short route to thwart the blitz. The quarterback adjusts his target and the "hot receiver" adjusts his route. If a quarterback at the line of scrimmage reads the defense and recognizes a blitz coming, he may call an audible to designate a receiver as a hot read or hot receiver.

HUDDLE

The groupings of offensive and defensive players to strategize before each play; the offensive team's huddle is almost always led by the quarterback, and the defensive huddle is typically led by one of the linebackers.

HUNG OUT TO DRY

A receiver put in a vulnerable position by a pass from his quarterback who has failed to consider the defenders converging on the receiver as the ball's in the air. A receiver in this situation is

Continued on page 54

SIDELINES: FANCY FOOTWORK

Feet are the tools of the trade for a football player. It's not just brute strength that's important on the field. Players often emulate ballet stars as they launch themselves in the air, pirouette, and catch a pass. When executed perfectly, these maneuvers give players an advantage over the opposition by using angles, not power.

BUCKET STEP OR KICK STEP

A 6-inch step backward where the lineman opens his hips. It is used for an outside zone play or when the blocker is uncovered.

DRIVE STEP

The player steps into the opponent, usually used for base blocking. The play-side foot always steps first.

DROP STEP

A step backward at a 45-degree angle and 6 inches horizontally. Used on an outside zone play when the defender is on the outside shade.

LEAD STEP (ZONE STEP)

A 45-degree angle, 6-inch step used mainly for the inside zone play. Designed to help get in front of the defender when he is shaded toward the play side.

SLIDE STEP

A 6-inch horizontal step toward the play side used for outside zone plays when the defender is head up to the blocker.

ZIGZAG RUN

Sprinting with an abrupt change of direction.

Continued from page 51

overly exposed to pursuing tacklers—injuries to
the pass catcher on such a play can often occur.

ICING THE KICKER

When a team calls a timeout or a succession of
timeouts to jar or rattle the opposing kicker as he
is about to attempt a field goal at a critical point in
a game, either near the end of play or as the first
half comes to a close.

INELIGIBLE RECEIVER

Certain players on the offense are not allowed to
catch passes. In most situations offensive interior
linemen can't be receivers and they may cause
their team to be penalized if they catch the ball.
An exception to this is if the ball has already been
touched by a different player.

INFLUENCE BLOCK

A reverse-psychology block where the player
pretends to block the defender as if the play was
a pass when it is really a run or vice versa. Or
the player pretends to block him in one direction
when he actually wants to block him in the other
direction. A good defender will react quickly to

and fight through the block, but his reaction will be incorrect since the block is "incorrect," albeit deliberately so. This maneuver works best against a well-coached, disciplined team.

ICING THE KICKER

INSIDE HANDOFF
When the ball is handed off to a runner who moves between the center, guards, and tackles at the line of scrimmage.

INSIDE-OUT PURSUIT
When one or two defenders (usually linebackers) lag a yard or so inside a ball carrier and run wide to stop his cutbacks. This one is no trivial pursuit.

INSIDE TRAP
A misdirection play on offense that traps a defender into committing early on the play and getting "trapped" out of position, thus enabling the ball carrier to find daylight instead of an awaiting tackler.

INTENTIONAL GROUNDING
A penalty against the quarterback when he throws the ball while inside the pocket to an area of the field without a receiver in it. He does this to avoid being sacked. This is a 10-yard penalty and results in a loss of down.

INSIDE TRAP

SIDELINES: WACKY END ZONE DANCES AND CELEBRATIONS

LAMBEAU LEAP

The Lambeau Leap is a legendary touchdown celebration that has actually been deemed legal even as the NFL punishes other such celebrations. After a touchdown the player vaults into the stands over the wall of the storied Lambeau Field that divides spectators from players, and is then mobbed by exuberant fans. Surprisingly, a defensive player, strong safety LeRoy Butler, performed the original Lambeau Leap on December 26, 1993, in a game against the Los Angeles Raiders. The ball bounced into the hands of Hall of Fame defensive end Reggie White,

who headed toward the end zone. Just as he was being tackled, White looked over and flipped the ball to Butler who completed a touchdown, then took off toward the crowd. Butler fell short of getting his hips over the edge of the wall, but several good-natured fans hoisted him into the stands. The commissioner, Paul Tagliabue, grandfathered the Lambeau Leap in as a legal celebration because the action doesn't show up the other team. He believed it conveys that the fans are actually appreciated for being part of the game. Thus, a tradition was born.

One player stated that the Leap looks easy to pull off—that is, until you try it the first time. His advice is to cover your privates and have somebody help you down.

JOE HORN, CALL HOME

Joe Horn, the New Orleans Saints' receiver, celebrated his second touchdown in a game against the New York Giants in 2003 (in which he would go on to score four) by pulling out a cell phone from underneath the goalpost padding.

He pretended to make a call to his mother. His little prank proved to be an expensive one: a 15-yard penalty for unsportsmanlike conduct and a $30,000 fine by the NFL.

KING OF END ZONE CELEBRATIONS

Former NFL wide receiver Terrell Owens is one of the best-known experts of the end-zone celebration. He has pulled a marker from his sock and autographed the ball, performed a series of sit-ups, mocked the touchdown dance of the Baltimore Ravens' Ray Lewis, and borrowed pom-poms from a cheerleader to cheer himself on.

INTERFERENCE

A penalty against either an offensive receiver or a defensive coverage player, if they bump each other while a pass is in the air.

INTERIOR LINE

These are offensive centers, guards, and tackles.

INVERT

Assigning cornerbacks to shallow pass responsibilities. Normally cornerbacks cover deep passes; when inverted, they cover shallow passes to the flat. Also called "cloud coverage" when referring to pass defense.

ISO

Short for isolation play. The fullback is isolated to block the linebacker at the play's focal point, with the running back following closely behind in an attempt to gain yardage. The other players who are lined up along the offensive line block the player opposite them, with two players blocking one opposing player at the point of play. Properly executed, this play can change from short yardage to game-breaker status in a split second. Lead play.

JAB STEP

A quick open step away from the direction that the offensive back plans to go on the play. Used to misdirect or sucker one or more defenders.

JAB STEP

KEY

What and who a defensive player looks at before
the snap of the ball. The defensive lineman must
key (watch) the offensive lineman and be prepared
to react to his movements. Typically all defenders
do this on designated offensive players related to
their defensive responsibilities. Two defenders
are the dive key and pitch key for the quarterback
when he runs a triple-option play.

KICK-OUT BLOCK

A block made on a running play by a blocker,
either on the offensive line or in the backfield
while running parallel to the line of scrimmage,
to kick an opponent out of the play. The kick-out
blocker must keep the outside edge rusher from
crashing to the inside. A fullback or pulling guard
normally does this play. Opposite of a crackback
block.

KNEEL DOWN

When a player (usually the quarterback) kneels
with the ball, he is performing a procedural
counterpart of being tackled with the ball—
instead of actually being tackled. According

to NFL rules, he is allowed to simulate being tackled by voluntarily kneeling. Ordinarily done to exhaust the game clock either near the end of the first half or as the game is coming to a close. When a quarterback kneels with the ball that play is over and the ball is set up for the next play. Also called taking a knee.

KICK-OUT BLOCK

LEAD

LANE

The area of responsibility of a member of a punt or kickoff team. The width of the lane is the width of the field divided by the number of kick team members assigned to lanes; or the area of responsibility of a member of the defensive line or linebacker during an apparent drop-back pass play to prevent a draw play.

LEAD

Offensive play when a fullback goes through a bubble to block a linebacker followed by a ball carrier. Also called an isolation, or iso, and blast play.

LEAD OPTION

A type of option play in which an offensive back goes around the end ahead of the ball carrier to block for him.

LEFT GUARD AND RIGHT GUARD

The inner two members of the offensive line. Their job is to block for and protect the quarterback and ball carriers.

LEFT TACKLE AND RIGHT TACKLE

The outer two members of the offensive line. Offensive tackle and defensive tackle are separate positions. The offensive tackle's job is to block. The right tackle, or RT, is the team's best blocker. The left tackle, or LT, is the team's best pass blocker. Defensive tackles are the largest and strongest of defensive players.

LEG WHIP

A tripping ploy in which a player on the ground swings his leg at another player in an illegal attempt to make a tackle or block. Results in a 15-yard penalty when caught by the officials.

LENGTHEN THE GAME

To stop the clock as much as possible in order to increase the number of plays in the game.

LID

Helmet.

LID

SIDELINES: LONGEST FIELD GOAL—WHAT A FEAT!

A player with half a foot accomplished the longest field goal in professional football. On November 8, 1973, twenty-two-year-old Tom Dempsey, of the New Orleans Saints, was brought into the game against the Detroit Lions as they led the game 17–16 with two seconds left. Dempsey, who had been born with half a foot, launched the ball an unheard of 63 yards to win the game for the Saints.

LINEBACKER

A defender who normally aligns "in the box" several yards off the line of scrimmage but aligns outside the box when he is assigned to cover a receiver other than the tight end.

LINE CALL

A verbal blocking instruction given by one offensive lineman or by the quarterback to other offensive linemen while they are at the line of scrimmage just before the snap. Used to adapt to unanticipated defensive alignments or to adjust to a defense that uses multiple alignments during a game. Close kin to the audible at the line of scrimmage.

LINE OF SCRIMMAGE, OR LOS

Line parallel to the yard lines that stretches all the way across the field and passes through the forward tip of the football before it is snapped. The starting point of the count off of remaining yards needed for first down.

LINE SPLITS

Distance between feet of neighboring offensive

linemen. Some offenses such as the single wing and double wing commonly use zero line splits—that is, the feet of adjacent linemen touch each other before the snap. Other offenses, most notably the triple option and the spread, use wide splits based on the theory that it enables their offensive linemen to simply maintain a hole that existed before the snap, which is easier than trying to make a hole, especially when your team is overmatched by the defense. Some modern pass-oriented offenses, most notably Texas Tech's in the 2000s, have huge offensive line splits.

LINE TO GAIN

Yard line the offense must get the ball across for a first down.

LIVE COLOR

Calling out a different color plus a play, the quarterback at the line of scrimmage gives the color as mnemonic for the play that will be run next. Colors and numbers are often used in combination, such as "Blue 12" and "Red 82," for many reasons. Sometimes the phrase indicates an audible and other times it helps players with their

LOAF

blocking assignments. Usually it will put a receiver in motion or just designate when the ball is about to be snapped.

LOAF

Not applying 100 percent of effort. Usually used to describe selfish or poorly conditioned players who are not the focal point of the play in question. Taking a play off.

LOAF AND LEAVE

When the receiver releases slowly off the line of scrimmage at the snap, as if he is not involved in this play, then accelerates to full speed on a streak route.

LOG

Type of block; a plan B of a trap block. If the blocker can't block the target outward, he blocks him inward instead. Occurs when the defender in question does a good job of squeezing the hole, thereby preventing the trap blocker from getting an inside position on him.

SIDELINES: WHAT IS FANTASY FOOTBALL?

A popular, fast-growing fan sport where participants ("team owners") choose actual NFL players for fictional teams and compete using scoring based on the players' statistics. Team owners decide which of their players' scores will count for each matchup by "starting" some in the "starting lineup" and "sitting" the rest on the "bench." Team owners try to improve their "roster" between matchups by trading players with other teams or adding players from the pool of the unselected. The "season" begins when team owners "draft" teams. And it ends after a period of regular matchups, playoffs, and a championship game.

Here's a little lingo:

BENCH PLAYERS: Owners choose not to start these players and generally receive no points for their performances.

BUST: A player who is expected to have a poor season. He might be injury-prone, have a future star behind him in the lineup, or simply won't be able to live up to the hype.

CUT OR DROP: To remove a player from your roster.

FF OR FFB: Short for Fantasy Football.

HANDCUFF: A backup player (primarily running backs) who will probably take over for a team's starter in case there is an emergency or injury. A common strategy on draft day is to stockpile several backups of prominent running backs who have been drafted.

SERPENTINE DRAFT OR SNAKE DRAFT: Each fantasy coach has one pick in each round. Every team makes its first-round pick based on a predetermined order. When the first round is over, the team that picked last in the first round picks first in the second round and the team that had the first pick in the first round now has the last pick in the second round, and so on. This process is commonly used because it allows for a fair and balanced draft.

SLEEPER: A draft term for an NFL player that an owner believes is going to have a breakout season. This doesn't necessarily always apply to rookies, but can include lesser-known players. Frequently sleepers are drafted in the middle to late rounds of a draft.

SIDELINES: PLAYERS' NICKNAMES

WALTER PAYTON, one of the most productive running backs in the history of the NFL, was given his nickname "Sweetness" by teammates in the Senior Bowl college all-star game. He was never sure whether his nickname referred to his sweet movements on the field or to his sweet, sincere personality and high-pitched voice. He first began to attract attention as a halfback at Jackson State University, making the starting lineup in 1971—his freshman year. Once he became a professional player in 1975 he continued to excel. Picked by the Chicago Bears, he became a running back who was known for his speed. During his thirteen seasons with the team, Payton made nine Pro Bowl appearances and won MVP twice—in 1977 and 1985.

LONG COUNT

Extremely long pre-snap cadence customarily used in a third-down-and-five-or-less situation when the defense is not expecting it. The play is designed to draw the opposing defense offsides. This play is more likely to work when used on an earlier down.

LONG SNAP

A snap where the ball travels at least 4 yards and as many as 18 yards on a line-drive trajectory, usually made to the quarterback in the shotgun formation, or to the punter, or to the holder for placekicks.

LONG SNAPPER

A specialist who only snaps for field goals and punts. This is such a valuable position that colleges recruit and pro teams hire players solely for this ability.

LONG YARDAGE

A behind-schedule down-and-distance combination. Some ideal down-and-distance templates would be: second and six, third and two, and fourth and one. "Long yardage" is the combining of those downs with greater distances. Plays used in such situations are likely to include passes and runs with big gain potential like draws and counters.

LONG SNAPPER

SIDELINES: FOOTBALL'S BEGINNINGS

In the United States, the sport that we know of as football is more correctly called gridiron football, because of the vertical yard lines that mark the field. British rugby and soccer are the two sports most closely aligned to gridiron football, which originated at universities in North America, primarily the United States, in the late nineteenth century.

On November 6, 1869, players from Princeton and Rutgers held the first intercollegiate football contest in New Brunswick, New Jersey, playing

a soccer-style game with rules adapted from the London Football Association. In the 1870s many other elite Northeastern colleges took up the sport. Harvard University introduced a rugby-soccer hybrid called the "Boston Game." In May 1874, after a match against McGill University of Montreal, the Harvard players decided they preferred McGill's rugby-style rules to their own.

In 1875, Harvard and Yale played their first intercollegiate match, and Yale players and spectators (including Princeton students) embraced the rugby style as well. Walter Camp, a Yale undergraduate and medical student from 1876 to 1881 who played halfback and served as team captain, was responsible for the transition from this rugby-like game to the football we know today. He is known as the "father of American football."

Camp, who coached, played, and wrote extensively on football, was the guiding force on the rules board of the newly formed Intercollegiate Football Association (IFA). The

IFA made two key improvements to the newly minted game, thanks to Camp. It did away with the opening "scrummage" or "scrum" and began requiring that a team give up the ball after failing to move down the field a specified yardage in a certain number of "downs." In addition, Camp introduced the eleven-man team, the quarterback position, the line of scrimmage, offensive signal calling, and the scoring scale used in football today. He also coached the Yale team to a 67–2 record from 1888 to 1892—all while working as an executive at the Haven Clock Company, a family firm.

LOOK-IN

A slant pass route with no "stem"—that is, a push upfield—when the receiver runs inside at a 45-degree angle starting on his first step after the snap.

LOOK IN AND TUCK

A drill where the receiver is supposed to keep his eyes on the ball until he has secured it into the ball-carrying position.

LOOP

A defensive stunt where a linebacker blitzes through a gap that is one or two gaps away from where he was aligned before the snap.

MOVE THE CHAINS

When a team gets a first down.

MUFF

The drop point of a punt that was never under control by the player attempting to field it. Not classified as a fumble, thus the ball cannot be advanced by the recovering team.

NAKED BOOTLEG

A running play where all the blockers run in one direction ahead of the flow of the play, including three of the four players in the backfield, while the quarterback carries the ball running "naked"—that is, without accompanying protection as he runs—in the opposite direction.

NICKEL

A defensive formation where the defense removes a linebacker and puts a fifth defensive back on the field in his place. Used in obvious passing situations such as third and long.

NICKELBACK

The cornerback or safety that functions as the fifth (in addition to the typical four) defensive back on the defense. A base defense contains four defensive backs, consisting of two cornerbacks and two safeties. Not a type of refund.

OFFSIDES

A foul in which a player is on the wrong side of the line of scrimmage when the ball is snapped. Occurs concurrently with the snap. Defensive

PANCAKE

players, unlike offensive players, are not required to come to a set position before the snap. If a defender jumps across the line but gets back to his side before the snap, there is no foul. In the case of an offside foul, play is not stopped, and the foul is announced at the conclusion of the play. This foul is nearly always committed by the defense. An offensive player moving into the neutral zone after setting would be charged with a false start. Yet, the offense could commit this foul. If an offensive player lines up in the neutral zone, an offside foul will be called against the offense. The penalty for violation is 5 yards.

PANCAKE

A forceful block, usually by the offensive linemen, tight end, or fullback that sets an opposing lineman completely on his back, taking him out of play. Not a breakfast, but could be a fast break.

PAT

Point after touchdown. One point if the ball is placekicked through two uprights, two if the ball is rushed or thrown and received in the end zone. The PAT begins on the 2-yard line.

SIDELINES: THE PIGSKIN?

Originally footballs were made out of animal bladders—sometimes the bladder of a pig, which is thought to be how the nickname "pigskin" came about. Animal bladders were much more accessible to the average team than more expensive items like leather. When the bladder was inflated, it was mostly round and served well as a ball for gameplay. Today NFL footballs are made of cowhide in a factory located in Ada, Ohio. Approximately 600 cows are needed to provide the leather for the number of footballs that are used in a season. Ambitious cows should be aware that their chances of winding up in a Super Bowl game have been calculated at 1 in 17,420,000!

SIDELINES: PLAYERS' NICKNAMES

RON JAWORKSI, a former quarterback who played for the Los Angeles Rams, Philadelphia Eagles, Miami Dolphins, and the Kansas City Chiefs. He was nicknamed "Jaws" by Doug Collins, a Philadelphia 76ers player and later coach, prior to the 1981 Super Bowl as he was always talking. During his younger days, he went by the name of "The Polish Rifle" or "The Polish Cannon" for being able to regularly fire passes.

ROGER STAUBACH, one of the most electrifying NFL players of the 1970s, was known as "Roger the Dodger" for his scrambling abilities, "Captain America" as quarterback for the Dallas Cowboys, America's Team, and also as "Captain Comeback" for his fourth-quarter game-winning heroics.

PICK

An illegal play that occurs when an offensive player tries to obstruct the progress or impedes the coverage of a downfield defender in order to allow a teammate to get open for a pass. Usually two receivers run a crossing pattern past each other with one receiver chosen to make enough contact with the defender to allow the other receiver to come open. If the official determines the contact to be deliberate or egregious, he can throw a flag for offensive pass interference. A common play and a technique that necessitates a team to design plays that can cause a pick without the flag being thrown for pass interference. Often, the picking player will have to manage to impede the defender's progress just enough to slow him down while not making the contact obvious enough to draw the flag. Most crossing patterns are designed to put players in positions that can create traffic thereby causing a pick situation without the obvious pick occurring.

PICK-SIX

An interception returned by the defense for a touchdown. If the quarterback passes the ball and a defender catches it, and "takes it to the house" (end zone), he has run in a "pick-six."

PIGSKIN
The football.

PIGSKIN

SIDELINES: HOW COULD HE LET THIS HAPPEN?

Late in the fourth quarter during Super Bowl XXVII on January 31, 1993, former Cowboys defensive tackle Leon Lett recovered a fumble on the Dallas 35-yard line and ran it back toward the end zone. When he reached the 10-yard line, Lett slowed and held the ball out as he continued toward the goal line. Unfortunately he didn't see Bills' wide receiver Don Beebe pursuing him from behind. Beebe whacked the ball out of Lett's outstretched hand just before he crossed the goal line, which propelled the ball through the end zone, resulting in a touchback that cost Lett his touchdown. When later asked about this blunder Lett said he had been watching the Jumbotron and was trying to do a "Michael Irvin," where he put the ball out across the goal line. The play is viewed as not having significantly affected the outcome of the game—the Cowboys had an impressive 52–17 lead at the time—but it humiliated Lett and is still talked about today. Lett's blooper also cost the Cowboys the record for most points scored in a Super Bowl (which is held by the San Francisco 49ers at 55 during Super Bowl XXIV).

PIGSKIN WITH MOHAWK

Still the football. The mohawk is the laces.

PISTOL OFFENSE

Commonly referred to as the "pistol formation," a versatile configuration and strategy, particularly if the quarterback himself is a threat to run the ball, which makes it difficult for the defense to correctly anticipate the play. The quarterback lines up 4 yards behind the center, much closer than the 7-yard setback in a traditional shotgun formation. The running back then lines up 3 yards directly behind the quarterback, which is in contrast to the shotgun, where they are beside each other. The position of the quarterback in this formation has an advantage: The quarterback is close enough to the line of scrimmage to be able to read the defense, as with run situation sets—such as the I formation—but far enough back to give him extra time and a better vision of the field for passing plays, as in the shotgun. Developed by Chris Ault in 2005 when he was head coach at the University of Nevada.

POOCH KICK

PLAY ACTION

When the quarterback fakes a handoff to the running back, making the defense believe it is a running play for the purpose of neutralizing a defense momentarily while allowing the receivers a split-second advantage for getting open.

POCKET

The area where the quarterback stands while protected by his linesmen as he looks to throw the ball downfield. If the offensive linemen don't properly block, then the pocket will collapse.

POOCH KICK

An intentional short punt when the offense is too far away from the uprights to attempt a field goal, but too close to where a normal full punt would land in the end zone and cause the football to be brought out to the 20-yard line on the change of possession, thus producing minimal net yardage for the punt. Similar to a coffin corner punt, except that the ball remains in bounds to be covered by the kicking team or taken as a fair catch by the returning team.

PUMP-FAKE

When a quarterback goes through a throwing motion but doesn't release the ball. Instead he uses this to neutralize a defense so that he might throw to another receiver, who has become open while the defense was reacting to the pump-fake, or he hands the ball off on a delay, or runs it himself on a designed play.

PUNT

A kick used by the offensive team to surrender possession of the ball if the team has not gained the yardage needed for a first down.

PUNTER

A specialist and special teams player who receives the snapped ball (commonly on the fourth down) directly from the line of scrimmage and then kicks (punts) the football to the opposing team. Sometimes punters also take part in fake punts in those same situations, when they throw or run the football instead of punting in hopes of gaining a first down and having their team retain possession of the ball and continue a drive toward the end zone.

SIDELINES: A WING AND A PRAYER

The term Hail Mary became well-known after a
December 28, 1975, NFL playoff game between
the Dallas Cowboys and the Minnesota Vikings.
Roger Staubach, the Cowboys quarterback and
a Roman Catholic, said about his game-winning
touchdown pass to wide receiver Drew Pearson,
"I closed my eyes and said a Hail Mary."

However, it was two former members of Notre
Dame's Four Horsemen, Noble Kizer and Jim

Crowley, who reportedly first used the expression. In public speeches Crowley often talked about an October 28, 1922, game between Notre Dame and Georgia Tech when the Notre Dame players said Hail Mary prayers together before scoring each of the touchdowns, winning the game 13–3. Crowley said it was Kizer, a Presbyterian, and one of the team's linemen, who encouraged praying before the first touchdown, which happened on a fourth and goal play at Tech's 6-yard line during the second quarter. Quarterback Harry Stuhldreher, another of the Horsemen, threw a quick pass over the middle to Paul Castner for the score. This was repeated before a third and goal play, again at Tech's six, in the fourth quarter. This time Stuhldreher ran for a touchdown, clinching the win for Notre Dame. After the game, Kizer reportedly shouted to Crowley, "That Hail Mary is the best play we've got."

Thirteen years later, on November 2, 1935, with only thirty-two seconds left in the alleged "Game of the Century" between Ohio State and Notre Dame, Irish halfback Bill Shakespeare located receiver Wayne Millner for a 19-yard game-winning touchdown. Notre Dame head coach Elmer Layden—who was also a player in the 1922 Georgia Tech game—afterward called it a "Hail Mary" play.

The first press reference to a Hail Mary pass was in a 1941 Associated Press article about the impending 1941 Orange Bowl between the Mississippi State Bulldogs and the Georgetown Hoyas. The piece appeared in several newspapers including the December 31, 1940, *Daytona Beach Morning Journal* under the headline "Orange Bowl: [Georgetown] Hoyas Put Faith in 'Hail Mary' Pass." The writer of the article clarified, "A 'Hail Mary' pass, in the talk of the Washington eleven, is one that is thrown with a prayer because the odds against completion are big."

PYLON

The typically orange marker indicating each of the four corners of the end zone. If the ball carrier makes contact with a pylon before going out of bounds on a running play a touchdown is scored even if the carrier never touches any other part of the end zone. This is considered "breaking the plane" of the end zone.

QUARTERBACK

The leader of the team. He calls the plays in the huddle, shouts the signals at the line of scrimmage, and receives the ball from the center. Then he hands the ball off to a running back, throws it to a receiver, or runs with it.

QUARTERBACK SNEAK

When the quarterback tries to gain short yardage by keeping the ball and running it forward. Usually used when the offense needs less than a yard to convert a first down.

QUICK OUT

A route where the receiver runs downfield, breaks sharply toward the sideline, and then looks for the ball. The opposite of a drag or in route.

QUICK SNAP

When the center gives the ball to the quarterback instantly upon the offense setting up rather than letting the quarterback go through his cadence.

RED ZONE

The area from the defense's 20-yard line to the goal line. The field is condensed, so it is harder to score a touchdown because a team's offensive system is often compacted when playing within that area. However, scoring can also be easier because the goal line is closer.

RED ZONE

SIDELINES: SMALLEST NFL PLAYER

Five-foot-one-and-a-half-inch-tall Jack Shapiro, of the 1929 Staten Island Stapletons, may also have had the shortest career: one game. Shapiro, who was also the shortest player in the NFL, had lettered in varsity football at NYU after joining as a walk-on. At a Thanksgiving game where Staten Island faced off against the Minneapolis Red Jackets, Shapiro played as a blocking back as the Stapletons went on to win 34–0. It was later revealed that he was signed as a publicity stunt: The Stapletons wanted to sell tickets for their game and draw a crowd to see their diminutive blocking back.

LARGEST PLAYERS IN THE NFL

Height: Richard Slight—Defensive tackle for the Oakland Raiders: 7 feet.
Weight: Michael Jasper—Offensive tackle and nose guard for the New York Giants: 448 pounds.

REVERSE

An offensive play with multiple handoffs. The quarterback gives the ball to a carrier running in one direction who then hands the ball to a carrier running in the opposite direction. On occasion there is a third handoff—with the ball returned to the quarterback, who then throws a pass to a receiver far downfield. A trick play.

ROLLOUT

Part of an offensive play when the quarterback runs to one side of the offensive backfield looking to pass the ball. Often used to run away from defensive pursuit.

RUNNING BACK

One of the more exciting positions on the field and considered by many to be one of the two most important people on the offense. Commonly viewed as an essential component for a team's success. His jobs are manifold. For instance, if the quarterback calls a running play, he hands the ball to the running back who then has the job of finding a hole in the defense and trying to reach the end zone as fast as he can.

Also, if the quarterback calls a passing play, the running back frequently has the job of staying near his quarterback for a second or two and blocking any defensive players who make it past the offensive line. And finally, the running back is often sent out as an additional receiver. Also known as ball carriers, fullbacks, halfbacks, rushers, and tailbacks.

SACK
Tackle of the quarterback behind the line of scrimmage for loss of yardage.

SAFETY
The players who line up the deepest in the secondary—the last line of defense.

SHORT SNAPPER
The center, and possibly a specialist, who snaps the ball for extra points or field goals.

SHOTGUN
An offensive formation where the quarterback stands farther behind the line of scrimmage, often 5 to 7 yards back, and receives the snap from the

center. Sometimes the quarterback will have a back on one or both sides before the snap, while other times he will be the lone player in the backfield, with everyone spread out as receivers. Advantages to using this formation are: If the defense has been using a lot of blitz packages or is bringing pressure on the quarterback, the shotgun gives the quarterback more room to make a pass. Also, since the shotgun indicates a pass play, a mobile quarterback can get the upper hand by using the extra time to scramble and gain yards before defensive backs are forced to close and make a tackle.

Disadvantages: The defense will be aware that a pass play is likely. Since the snap is longer there's more risk of a bungled snap, leading to a possible turnover or loss of yards. Also, any defensive pass rushers penetrating the offensive line will have less traffic to move through on their way to the quarterback, making a sack or tackle for loss more probable. Teams that prefer or feature passing over running often use the shotgun formation on a regular basis.

SIDELINE

The out-of-bounds line down each side of the playing field. Also refers to the out-of-bounds area outside the playing field where the coaches and substitutes observe the game.

SLOBBER KNOCKER

A firm, hard hit where one can see spittle fly from the mouth of a player.

SLOBBER KNOCKER

SNAP

The backward passing of the ball at the start of play from scrimmage. Also called a hike, pass from center, or snapback.

SPIKE

A play when the quarterback deliberately throws the ball at the ground immediately after the snap. Technically it is an incomplete pass, and therefore has the effect of stopping the clock and exhausting a down. Used when the offensive team is steering a hurried drive near the end of the first half of the game, and the game clock is still running in the aftermath of the previous play. As an incomplete pass this play causes the referee to stop the game clock, and the offensive team then has a chance to huddle and plan the next play without losing scarce game-clock time. Also known as clocking the ball.

This maneuver is not considered intentional grounding and no penalty is assessed if the play is done with the quarterback under center and immediately after the snap. The only loss is that one down is sacrificed.

Running this play assumes there will be one play (at the very least) by the same team immediately afterward. Consequently it would not be completed on fourth down; instead, a regular play would have to be run without a huddle.

STATUE OF LIBERTY

The most common variation of this highly deceptive, high-yardage trick play involves the quarterback taking the snap from the center, dropping back, and holding the ball with two hands as if he were to throw. He then places the ball behind his back with his non-throwing hand while standing in the pocket at an angle (resembling the Statue of Liberty), which conceals his deceit, then pump-faking a throw to one side of the field. While his arm is still in motion during the fake throw, he hands the ball off behind his back to a running back or a wide receiver who then runs the football to the opposite side of the field. The objective is to trick the defense out of position, leaving them unable to catch up with the runner as he sprints in the direction opposite to the fake.

STATUE OF LIBERTY

TACKLE BOX

The area between where the two offensive tackles line up prior to the snap.

THREE AND OUT

After starting an offensive possession, a team executes three plays and fails to get a first down, forcing them to punt or, if close enough, attempt a field goal.

Derives from the standard practice that an offensive unit has only three "real" plays before they are expected to punt. A team is allowed a fourth play in principle but this typically is not used. Exercising the fourth down to execute a play is a chancy move under most circumstances. If a team fails to convert to a new first down on a fourth-down play, the opposing team will then be permitted to take over possession at the stop where they left off. This gives them better field position than if the ball is punted farther toward the opposing team's end zone. Usually, a team will only attempt a play on a fourth-down if they are trailing late in a close game, are near enough to the first-down marker (usually a yard or less) and in the opposing team's territory, or are deep enough where a punt likely results in a touchback, but just out of field-goal range.

Punting following a three-and-out is unlike a turnover on downs. Punting after a three-and-out gives a team the chance to set their opposition farther back in field position. On a turnover on downs there is no punt, and the opposing team takes over possession of the ball at the spot of field where the fourth down attempt failed.

THREE YARDS AND A CLOUD OF DUST

This American football idiom is frequently attributed to the famous Ohio State University coach Woody Hayes. Instead of having his players throw a long pass and possibly gain many yards at a time, Hayes chose to have them keep the ball close to the ground and move in small increments, inexorably toward the opponents' goal line, one methodical first down after another until they culminated the drive with a touchdown.

THROUGH THE UPRIGHTS

Successful field goals.

THREE YARDS AND A CLOUD OF DUST

SIDELINES: MOST LOPSIDED NFL SCORE

When the 1940 NFL Championship Game ended between the Chicago Bears and the Washington Redskins, the Bears had scored a whopping 93 points while the Redskins had recorded 0. The Bears had eight interceptions and three of those were returned for a touchdown.

SIDELINES: PLAYERS' NICKNAMES

CHUCK BEDNARIK, the Philadephia Eagles' Hall of Fame center and linebacker who worked during his off-season as a salesman for a concrete company, was one of the last NFL players to play on both offense and defense. His nickname, "Concrete Charlie," suited him perfectly since he had an intimidating presence as a jolting blocker at center and as a crushing tackler at middle linebacker. Playing for the Eagles from 1949 to 1962, he missed only three games. Bednarik was notorious for flattening Frank Gifford, the late Giants' star in 1960, an action captured in an iconic photograph. A two-time All-American at Penn, he played in eight Pro Bowls and was elected to the Pro Football Hall of Fame in 1967. The NFL selected him as the center for its fiftieth-anniversary team in 1969, and he was elected that year to the College Football Hall of Fame. The Chuck Bednarik Award is presented annually to college football's best defensive player.

TIGHT END

A player who serves as a receiver and also as a blocker in almost equal measure. This player lines up beside the offensive tackle to the right or the left of the quarterback.

TOUCHBACK

A ruling signaled by an official when the ball becomes dead on or behind a team's own goal line (i.e., in an end zone) and the opposing team gave the ball the momentum, or incentive, to travel over or across the goal line. May be imparted by a kick, pass, fumble, or in certain instances by batting the ball. A touchback is not a play. Instead it is the result of events that may occur during a play. The opposite of a safety, a touchback is scored when the defending team is responsible for the ball becoming dead on or behind its own goal line.

VANILLA OFFENSE

An offense with few plays and/or formations. Named because vanilla flavoring is bland. Mostly used in exhibition games or college spring games to prevent opposing coaches from collecting any information from the team's playbook.

WILDCAT FORMATION

An offensive formation where the ball is not snapped to the nominal quarterback, but directly to a player of another position lined up where the quarterback might often be in the shotgun formation, usually a running back, though some playbooks have the wide receiver, fullback, or tight end taking the snap. Often characterized by an unbalanced offensive line that may look to the defense like a sweep is about to unfold behind zone blocking. A variation of the sweep by the direct snap's recipient usually results. Pass plays are infrequent from the wildcat formation, and hold out the element of surprise when a player who ordinarily wouldn't be throwing the football attempts a pass.

SIDELINES: MEMBERS OF THE CHAIN GANG

A "rod man" holds a pole (the "rear rod") that marks the beginning of the recent set of downs. A "box man" grasps a pole with an indicator of the current down at the top (the "box"). Another "rod man" grips a rod (the "forward rod") ten yards toward the defense's goal line from the rear rod man. This marker indicates a line on the

field—the "line to gain"—that the offense needs to reach in their series of four downs in order to retain possession of the ball. The two rods (occasionally known as "sticks") are attached at the bottom by a chain precisely 10 yards long. When the chain is taut, the rods are 10 yards apart.

The offices of the home team instead of the league or conference usually pick members of

the chain gang. In the NFL, members of the chain crew must have credentials permitting them access to the field. They are required to wear white shirts.

Unlike the players, the chain gang does not wear protective gear. A regular instruction by officials to the chain gang is to withdraw or drop their signals, and move back, if the play comes toward them and puts them at risk. The signals often use a bright orange color and are padded to decrease injuries.

All three poles are placed on the sidelines. For games at all levels below the NFL, the chain gang works on the side of the field opposite the press box and home team (the side of the visiting team). The chain gang switches sidelines at halftime in the NFL and the referee determines their initial placement. On fields where both teams' benches are located on the same side of the field, the chain gang operates on the opposite sideline for the whole game.

SIDELINES: PLAYERS' NICKNAMES

HAROLD EDWARD GRANGE: A college and professional halfback for the University of Illinois, the Chicago Bears, and for the short-lived New York Yankees was nicknamed "Red" at an early age because of his red hair. He was also known as "The Galloping Ghost" or "The Galloping Red Ghost." American sportswriter Warren Brown (who coined the "Sultan of Swat" for baseball legend Babe Ruth) gave Grange his nicknames when writing a column describing the halfback's running style, saying he was like a "Galloping Ghost." It is one of the most famous nicknames in sports annals.

ELROY HIRSCH, an American football running back and receiver for the Los Angeles Rams and Chicago Rockets, was nicknamed "Crazylegs" for his unusual running style; he looked like he was moving in six different directions as he shot down the field.

ZEBRA

The referee or other members of the officiating crew, who have the responsibility of enforcing the rules and upholding the order of the game. A referee wears a black-and-white-striped shirt, hence the nickname's popularity.

ZEBRA

ABOUT THE AUTHORS

SALLY COOK is the author, with James Charlton, of *How to Speak Baseball* and *Hey Batta Batta Swing! The Wild Old Days of Baseball,* illustrated by Ross MacDonald. She coauthored, with legendary football coach Gene Stallings, *Another Season: A Coach's Story of Raising an Exceptional Son,* a *New York Times* bestseller.

ROSS MACDONALD'S illustrations have appeared in *The New York Times, The New Yorker, Rolling Stone, Harper's, The Atlantic Monthly,* and *Vanity Fair.* He has also written and illustrated several books for children and adults. His most recent is *What Would Jesus Craft?*